THE
ICE CREAM
HANDBOOK

THE
ICE CREAM
HANDBOOK

VICKI SMALLWOOD

© 2005 D&S Books Ltd
© 2010 Kerswell Farm Ltd

This edition published by Kerswell Books Ltd

Printed 2010

This book is distributed in the UK by
Parkham Books Ltd
Kerswell Farm,
Parkham Ash, Bideford
Devon, England
EX39 5PR

enquiries@parkhambooks.co.uk

ISBN: 978-1-906239-59-6

DS0131. Ice Cream Handbook

Creative Director: Sarah King
Editor: Nicky Barber
Project Editor: Anna Southgate
Photographer: Colin Bowling/Paul Forrester
Designer: 2H Design

Printed in China

1 3 5 7 9 10 8 6 4 2

CONTENTS

INTRODUCTION

I ce cream is no longer a treat just for hot days and holidays; it is a round-the-year treat. Today, the choice of ice cream is vast and stretches across a broad selection of flavours and price ranges. This is not really surprising, as I think almost everyone likes ice cream of some sort, whether on its own or as an accompaniment. A scoop of ice cream melting into a slice of hot apple pie, or a simple but delicious bowl of vanilla ice cream, are wonderful ways to finish a meal. And ice cream can hold its own against a box of chocolates or sweets, as many people love to sit down to watch television with a bowl or even tub of their favourite ice cream.

Ice cream makers are now so readily available and easy to use that you can have delicious, freshly made ice cream or sorbet on the table in under an hour. You can be sure of the quality of home-made ice cream, which in this time of food scares and additive anxieties is a comforting thought. Ice cream or sorbet without additives can actually be a healthy indulgence! Compared with most shop-bought ice creams, sorbets and even flavoured yoghurts, many home-made ice creams and sorbets have less sugar per portion. Your ice cream can be as low-fat as you like, or dairy free if you prefer, and it will

be full of vitamins. People with food allergies can have ice creams and sorbets without the anxiety of triggering an allergic reaction. Buffalo or goats' milk and yoghurt are both good alternatives for many people with dairy allergies, and if those are not acceptable then you can always stick to sorbets which have no need for any dairy products. Many children will experiment with flavours in ice cream that they wouldn't normally try in other foods. In fact, if you have children, investing in an ice cream maker will pay off time and time again. There is no easier way of getting children to eat part of their daily fruit and calcium requirement.

Ice cream making is a fun way to interest children in cooking, and it doesn't take too much patience! The huge range of ice creams and sorbets will mean that the machine is kept busy with each member of the family wanting to make their favourite – leading on to the bolder members of the family experimenting with their own flavour combinations. Once you have got the hang of ice cream making, a delicious treat is never far away!

There are several types of ice cream maker available, ranging from manual versions to top-of-the-range automatic machines that have their own freezers. Of course, you can make ice cream by hand, but the texture is never quite as light or smooth as that of an ice cream made in a machine.

As you would expect, manual models are at the cheaper end of the market. They generally consist of a bowl that has to be placed in your freezer overnight. When the bowl has reached the correct temperature you remove it from the freezer and add your ingredients, fit the lid and paddles, and start to churn! Churning can take up to 30 minutes, so make sure you have plenty of arm power. If you stop, the ice cream in contact with the sides of the machine will freeze solid and so make it impossible to turn the

paddles! However, after all that work you have a ready-to-eat ice cream.

The next models up from the manual versions have electric motors fitted for churning. You still have to freeze the bowl overnight, but when you add the ingredients, fit the lid and flip the switch, the churning is done automatically. These and the manual models are relatively cheap and not particularly large, so can be stored quite easily, but you need to take into consideration the space required in the freezer as well as the planning-ahead factor, which for some can be a problem!

Top-of-the-range models have freezers as well as automatic churning. Needless to say they are not cheap, but it is worth investing in one of these models if you love ice cream and plan to make it often. All you do is pour in the ingredients and then turn the machine on, returning after approximately 30 minutes to find ice cream ready to serve.

Of course, you can always make ice cream by hand. The only requirements are a freezer that reaches –18°C or 0°F, shallow freezer-proof containers, and time. You simply have to remove the mixture from the freezer every 2 to 3 hours to whisk the ice crystals that form around the edges into the middle to make a kind of slush. You will need to do this at least 3 or 4 times in order to get a texture light enough to scoop.

As is so often the case, ice cream is best eaten freshly made. Contrary to popular belief, frozen foods do not keep indefinitely, and the taste will deteriorate after time. So to enjoy your ice cream at its best, eat within a week to ten days. You can leave it longer but the flavours just won't be as good after this time.

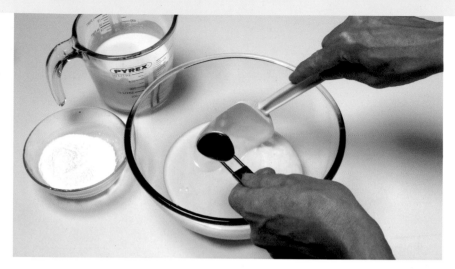

Tips for ice cream making

It is very important to read these tips and notes before starting to make any recipes in this book. Ice cream can be very easy to make, but there are a few rules that you must always abide by in order to guarantee successful results.

n   It is very important to keep everything scrupulously clean, as bacteria can thrive on the ingredients used in ice cream.

n   Never re-freeze ice cream that has defrosted.

n   All the eggs used in the recipes are medium size. I like to use organic or at least free-range eggs: quality is important for a good end result. Do not give undercooked or partly cooked eggs to young children, pregnant women or the elderly.

n   I recommend using UHT milk as it remains more stable for the making of custard-based ice creams. Always use full-fat milk: skimmed milk or low-fat milk is not suitable for ice creams.

n   When using liquid glucose, it will flow more easily if you stand the pot or jar in warm water for 2–3 minutes before using. Also, if possible, warm the spoon before measuring out the required amount.

14

n   All spoon measurements are level, unless otherwise stated.

n   All creams used in the recipes should be fresh, and all fruits should be ripe without any signs of deterioration.

n   Never switch between imperial and metric measurements when using a recipe: stick to one set of measurements from start to finish.

n   Never overfill your ice cream machine. You should probably only have the bowl two-thirds full if the machine does not have a fill guide on it. If this means that you have more mixture than will comfortably fit in your machine, just churn it in two batches, keeping the second batch in the fridge until the first is done.

n   If you don't have time to make the ice cream from start to finish, you can prepare the mixture in advance, cool it and keep it in the fridge for several hours before churning. This is not suitable for any of the ice creams that have fruit that can discolour – apples, bananas and pears.

n   If you have time, chill all your ingredients before adding to the machine, as this will shorten the churning time. If you don't have time, don't worry, just ensure that all ingredients are no warmer than room temperature.

n   Some ice creams will scoop straight from the freezer – this will depend on the ice cream and/or your freezer. But if the ice cream is too hard to serve straight away, allow it to stand for 2 to 3 minutes at room temperature, or alternatively leave it in the fridge for approximately 5 to 10 minutes.

n   When making any of the custards, it is best to use a wooden spoon for stirring over the heat. This is particularly good because it does not conduct heat, and is perfect for testing the thickness of the custard.

n   All recipes serve 4 to 6 people – depending on their appetites! Some people say that you need smaller portions of these ice creams as they are richer than commercially produced ones and they aren't full of air. But there are others who say that you need more!

n   If, after churning, the ice cream is still a little soft and you want it to be harder, simply scoop it into your freezer-proof containers and put it into the freezer for an hour or so to harden.

n   Do not boil the custard base as it may curdle. Heat to just below boiling point, stirring all the time to ensure even thickening, and then remove from the heat.

n   I recommend having a few stacking plastic boxes with lids for storing your ice creams in the freezer.

n   A freezer-proof pen and labels are also useful for ice cream storage

Toppings and extras!

Some might say that it is gilding the lily to add anything to a delicious
home-made ice cream. I will leave the choice of which ice creams can take
additions, and which are better served alone, up to you and your taste buds.
Most supermarkets stock a wide range of ice cream toppings, ranging from
sauces to wafers, biscuits and crunchy sprinkles. If you want to make your
own, I have included a few sauces and biscuits for you to try with your ice

creams. For sprinkling, why not try finely chopped dried fruits, sliced fresh fruits, broken biscuits, your favourite chocolate bar chopped up, toasted nuts, a spoonful of tinned fruits, lightly toasted cake crumbs or even a small packet of sweets. In much the same way, you can add similar ingredients at the end of churning, giving only two or three stirs to achieve a surprise ripple effect.

I hope you like the following recipes and that they give you the confidence to experiment with your own flavours. Enjoy!

COOL & CREAMY

Easy Custard

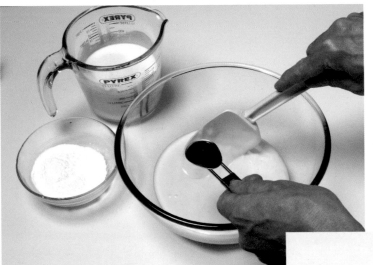

Ingredients

300ml/ ½ pt ready-made
  custard
300ml/ ½ pt double cream
25g/1oz icing sugar
1 teaspoon vanilla essence

Adding the vanilla essence.

Place the custard in a mixing bowl and add the vanilla essence, stirring well to mix. Add the cream and sift in the icing sugar. Stir well to mix. If you have time, chill the mixture for 3–4 hours to reduce the churning time. Use this mixture to make the ice cream according to the instructions of your ice cream maker.

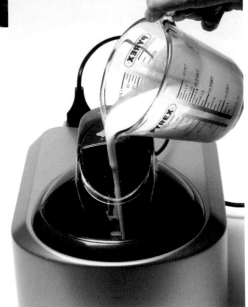

Pouring the mixture into the ice cream maker.

Store-cupboard Ice Cream

Chill the can of evaporated milk for 3–4 hours in the fridge. Then pour into a mixing bowl and whisk for approximately 4 minutes, or until the milk becomes thick and mousse-like. Sift the icing sugar and add to the milk along with vanilla essence, folding them in as gently as possible. Now use this mixture to make the ice cream according to the instructions of your ice cream maker. This ice cream is best served shortly after making.

Ingredients
410g/14-oz can evaporated milk
25g/1oz icing sugar
2 teaspoon vanilla essence

Whisking until mousse-like.

Folding in the icing sugar.

Coffee Ice Cream

Place the egg yolks and sugar in a large mixing bowl and whisk until the mixture becomes mousse-like. This will take approximately 5–8 minutes. Pour the milk into a saucepan and place over a gentle heat. Bring almost to the boil then remove from the heat and pour in a steady stream over the egg yolk and sugar mixture, whisking all the time. Return the mixture to the pan and cook over a gentle heat, stirring all the time with a wooden spoon until it thickens slightly. You can check the consistency by dipping a wooden spoon into the mixture then running your finger over the back of the spoon. If your finger leaves a clean trail then the mixture is ready. Leave to cool fully, then stir in the coffee and glucose. Following the instructions of your ice cream maker, use the mixture to make the ice cream.

Ingredients

4 egg yolks

100g/4oz Demerara sugar

450ml/ ¾pt milk

150ml/ ¼pt cold strong
    black coffee

2 tablespoons liquid glucose

Adding milk to the egg yolk and sugar mixture.

Pouring glycerine into the pan.

Vanilla

Using a sharp knife, split the vanilla pod lengthways. In a saucepan, gently heat the milk and vanilla pod until almost boiling then remove from the heat and set to one side to infuse for 30 minutes. Then remove the vanilla pod, scraping the inside of the pod with a knife and stirring this black paste into the milk – these are the vanilla seeds that will give the ice cream the distinctive speckled appearance of real vanilla. In a mixing bowl, whisk the egg yolks and sugar until pale and mousse-like. In a saucepan, gently heat the vanilla milk and creams until almost boiling then pour in a steady stream over the sugar and yolks, whisking as you do so. Return the mixture to the pan and cook, stirring all the time until the mixture thickens. You can check the consistency by

Ingredients

1 vanilla pod
150ml/ ¼ pt milk
6 egg yolks
100g/4oz caster sugar
150ml/ ¼ pt double cream
450ml/ ¾ pt single cream

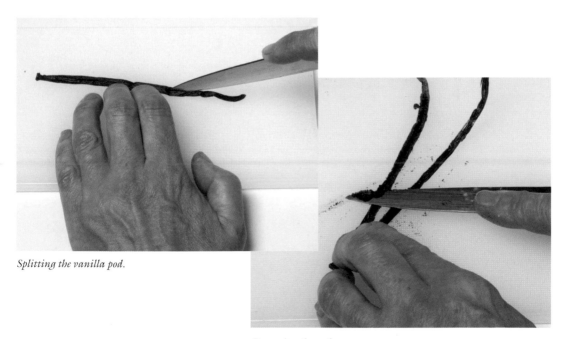

Splitting the vanilla pod.

Removing the seeds.

Whisk the egg yoks and sugar.

dipping a wooden spoon into the mixture then running your finger over the back of the spoon. If your finger leaves a clean trail then the mixture is ready. Set to one side to cool. Once fully cooled, use this custard to make your ice cream according to the instructions of your ice cream maker.

Stirring in the vanilla seeds.

Dulce de Lait

In a small pan, gently heat the milk and dulce de lait, stirring until they are fully combined. Remove from the heat and allow to cool. Once cooled, stir in the single and double cream, then following the instructions of your ice cream maker use this mixture to make the ice cream.

Ingredients

200g/7oz dulce de lait

150ml/ ¼ pt milk

150ml/ ¼ pt single cream

300ml/ ½ pt double cream

Heating the milk and dulce de lait.

If you want to make your own dulche de lait, take an unopened can of condensed milk and place in a large saucepan full of water. Bring to the boil, reduce the heat to a simmer and cover with a well fitting lid. Cook for an hour and 15 minutes checking regularly that the can is covered by the water. If you need to top up the water always add boiling water or you will slow down the cooking process. DO NOT ALLOW THE PAN TO BOIL DRY AS THE CAN COULD EXPLODE. Once the cooking time is up, remove from the heat and allow to cool fully before opening the can. Remove the contents of the can to a clean, airtight container, store in the fridge. Use as required – delicious on toast, as a cake filling, in pancakes and, of course, ice cream.

Stirring in the cream.

Mocha Ice Cream

Whisking the caster sugar and eggs.

Ingredients

6 egg yolks

75g/3oz caster sugar

250ml/9fl oz double cream

250ml/9fl oz milk

3 tablespoons cocoa
    powder, sifted

1 teaspoon espresso powder

In a large bowl, whisk the caster sugar and egg yolks
together until thick and mousse-like. Gently heat the milk
and cream in a saucepan. Place the cocoa and espresso
powder in a small bowl, add 1–2 tablespoons of the cream
mixture and stir to combine, ensuring that there are no
lumps. Add this mixture to the pan with the remaining cream
and milk and continue to cook until almost boiling. Remove
from the heat and pour in a steady stream over the sugar and
yolks, whisking as you do so. Return the mixture to the pan
and cook, stirring all the time until the mixture thickens. You
can check the consistency by dipping a wooden spoon into
the mixture then running your finger over the back of the
spoon. If your finger leaves a clean trail then the mixture is
ready. Leave to cool fully. Following the instructions of your
ice cream maker, use the mixture to make the ice cream

Adding cream to the cocoa and
espresso powder.

Real Coffee Ice Cream

Heat the milk until almost boiling then remove from the heat and pour over the coffee grounds. Set to one side to infuse. Once this mixture is cool, pour through a fine mesh sieve to remove the coffee, pressing down on the grounds with the back of a spoon to extract as much of the coffee-flavoured milk as possible. Discard the coffee grounds and set the flavoured milk to one side. In a saucepan dissolve the sugar in 150ml/ ¼ pt water, once the sugar has dissolved increase the heat and bring to the boil. Continue to boil until the syrup reaches 110°C/225°F on a sugar thermometer. Remove from the heat and allow to cool for 5 minutes. Add the syrup to the egg yolks in a thin steady stream, whisking all the time until the mixture becomes thick and mousse-like. Stir in the cream and coffee-flavoured milk. Allow to cool fully then use this mixture to make the ice cream following the instructions of your ice cream maker.

Ingredients
200ml/7fl oz milk
3 tablespoons ground
  coffee
100g/4oz granulated sugar
4 egg yolks
400ml/14fl oz double
  cream

Extracting the coffee-flavoured milk.

Adding the syrup to the egg yolks.

Kulfi

Pour the milk into a large saucepan. Split the cardamom pods by crushing them with a wooden spoon and add them to the milk. Bring the milk to the boil and then reduce the heat to a gentle simmer. Continue to cook the milk until it has reduced by approximately two-thirds, stirring every so often. If a skin forms, stir it back into the milk. This will probably take about 1½ hours, but you can't hurry it by turning up the heat, as you will only burn the milk. Once the milk has reduced and you have approximately 800ml/ 1⅓ pt remove from the heat, strain, and discard the cardamom pods. Add the sugar and stir until it has dissolved. Add the pistachios, then leave to cool. Once this mixture is cold, use it to make the ice cream following the instructions of your ice cream maker. When the ice cream is ready you can if you wish put it into moulds before placing in the freezer or serving.

Ingredients

21/4 ¼ pt whole milk
6 cardamom pods
75g/3oz caster sugar
50g/2oz pistachios,
   chopped

Splitting the cardamom pods.

Adding the pistachios.

FRUITY

Rhubarb & Custard

Ingredients
750g/1lb 10oz rhubarb,
  washed and cut into
  5cm/2in lengths
75g/3oz soft brown sugar
2 tablespoons cornflour
200ml/7fl oz milk
50g/2oz caster sugar
1 teaspoon vanilla extract

Cooking the rhubarb untill tender.

Making the cornflour mixture.

Place the rhubarb, soft brown sugar and 150ml/ 1/4 pt of water in a saucepan and cook until the rhubarb is tender. Set to one side and allow to cool. In a bowl, mix the cornflour with 2 tablespoons of the milk, then set to one side. Heat the remaining milk in a saucepan, with the caster sugar, until almost boiling. Pour one-third of the hot milk over the cornflour mixture, stirring all the time. Pour this mixture back into the saucepan and continue to cook, stirring continuously until the mixture thickens. Remove from the heat, add the vanilla essence and allow to cool fully, stirring from time to time to prevent a skin forming. Once fully cooled, mix the rhubarb and the custard together and following the instructions of your ice cream maker, use the mixture to make the ice cream.

Cherry Cream

Drain the juice from the cherries and pour into a pan – there should be about 300ml/ ½ pt. Bring to the boil and cook until the juice is reduced by about half. Remove from the heat and set to one side to cool. In a clean pan, gently heat the cream until almost boiling then remove from the heat and set to one side. In a mixing bowl, beat the egg yolks and sugar together until the mixture is thick. Continue beating as you pour in the hot cream in a steady stream. Once all the cream has been

Ingredients

470g/1lb 1oz cherries in
  syrup
300m/ ½ pt double cream
2 egg yolks
25g/1oz caster sugar

Reducing the juice by half.

45

incorporated return the mixture to the pan and cook, stirring all the time, over a gentle heat until the mixture has thickened. You can check the consistency by dipping a wooden spoon into the mixture then running your finger over the back of the spoon. If your finger leaves a clean trail then the mixture is ready. Leave to cool fully. Roughly chop the cherries in a blender or food processor and add the cooled reduced juice. Combine the fruit mixture and custard and, following the instructions of your ice cream maker, use the mixture to make the ice cream.

Chopping the cherries in a blender.

Rhubarb Crumble

Preheat the oven to 180°C/350°F/Gas mark 4. Wash the rhubarb and cut into 8cm/3in lengths. Place the rhubarb on a large baking tray and sprinkle over the granulated sugar and 1 tablespoon of water. Bake in the preheated oven for approximately 15 minutes, or until the rhubarb is tender. Put to one side to cool fully.

Whisk the caster sugar and egg yolks together in a large bowl until thick and mousse-like. Gently heat the milk and cream until almost boiling then pour in a steady stream over the sugar and yolks, whisking as you do so. Return the mixture to the pan and cook, stirring all the time, until the mixture thickens. You can check the consistency by dipping a wooden spoon into the mixture then running your finger over the back of the spoon. If your finger leaves a clean trail then the mixture is ready. Leave to cool fully.

Ingredients
400g/14oz rhubarb
1 tablespoon granulated
  sugar
4 egg yolks
50g/2oz caster sugar
250ml/9fl oz milk
250ml/9fl oz double cream
50g/2oz self raising flour
40g/1 ½ oz butter,
  chopped
40g/1 ½ oz Demerara
  sugar

Sprinkling sugar over the rhubarb.

In a mixing bowl, rub the butter into the flour until the mixture resembles coarse breadcrumbs then rub in the Demerara sugar. Sprinkle the mixture over a baking tray lined with baking parchment. Cook in the preheated oven for 10–15 minutes or until golden. Leave to cool fully before removing from the baking tray.

Mix the cooled rhubarb and custard mixture together then, following the instructions of your ice cream maker, use the mixture to make the ice cream. Sprinkle over some of the crumble mixture to serve. Alternatively you can add the crumble mixture for the final 2 minutes of the ice cream churning.

Baking the crumble mixture.

Coconut

Gently heat the coconut milk and condensed milk in a pan until almost boiling, stirring from time to time. Then remove from the heat and set to one side to cool fully. Once the mixture is completely cold, follow the instructions of your ice cream maker to make the ice cream.

Ingredients

500ml/18fl oz coconut
milk

200ml/7fl oz condensed
milk

Heating the condensed milk and coconut milk.

Pouring the mixture into an ice cream maker.

Coconut & Ginger

In a large bowl, whisk the soft brown sugar and egg yolks together until thick and mousse-like. Gently heat the milks together until almost boiling, then pour in a steady stream over the sugar and yolks, whisking as you do so. Return the mixture to the pan and cook, stirring all the time until the mixture thickens. You can check the consistency by dipping a wooden spoon into the mixture then running your finger over the back of the spoon. If your finger leaves a clean trail then the mixture is ready. Remove from the heat. Finely chop the stem ginger and stir into the custard. Then leave to cool fully before following the instructions of your ice cream maker to make the ice cream.

Ingredients

4 egg yolks

100g/4oz light soft brown sugar

300ml/ ½ pt coconut milk

300ml/ ½ pt milk

2 large pieces stem ginger

Chopping the stem ginger.

Whisking the egg yolks and soft brown sugar.

Blackcurrant

Drain the blackcurrants and pour the syrup into a pan, there should be about 300ml/ ½ pt. Bring to the boil and cook until the juice is reduced to about 150ml/ ¼ pt. Remove from the heat and set to one side to cool. In a clean pan, heat the milk and sugar together until the sugar has dissolved, then remove from the heat and set to one side to cool fully. Once cooled, combine the blackcurrants, reduced syrup, Greek yoghurt and milk mixture and, following the instructions of your ice cream maker, use the mixture to make the ice cream.

Ingredients

470g/1lb 1oz blackcurrants
  in syrup
3 tablespoons granulated
  sugar
150ml/ ¼ pt milk
300ml/ ½ pt Greek
  yoghurt

Heating the milk and sugar in a pan.

Combining the blackcurrants, syrup, milk and Greek yoghurt.

Blueberry & Goats' Milk

Place the blueberries and sugar in a large saucepan. Add 50ml/4tbsp water and cook, gently stirring from time to time, until the blueberries are soft and start to lose their shape. Set to one side to cool fully. Once cooled, stir in the yoghurt and, following the instructions of your ice cream maker, use the mixture to make the ice cream.

Heating the blueberries until soft.

Ingredients
350g/12oz blueberries
100g/4oz sugar
350g/12oz goats' milk
   yoghurt

Stirring in the yoghurt.

Strawberries & Cream

Ingredients
150ml/ ¼ pint double
   cream
100g/4oz condensed milk
575g/1 ¼ lb strawberries

Pouring the condensed milk into the pan.

Place the cream and condensed milk in a small pan and heat gently, stirring all the time, until almost boiling. Remove from the heat and set to one side to cool fully. Wash and hull the strawberries, then slice or roughly chop before blending to a purée in a liquidiser or food processor. Once the cream mixture has cooled, stir it into the strawberry purée and, following the instructions of your ice cream maker, use the mixture to make the ice cream.

Chopping the strawberries.

Pineapple & Coconut

Straining the coconut mixture.

Ingredients

400ml/14fl oz pineapple
juice
50g/2oz desiccated
coconut
432g/15-oz can pineapple
cubes in syrup
3 tablespoons liquid glucose

Heat the pineapple juice with the desiccated coconut until almost boiling then set to one side to cool. Strain, reserving the juice and discarding the coconut. Strain the pineapple cubes reserving the juice. Blend the pineapple cubes until smooth and then add to the coconut-flavoured juice, along with the glucose. Stir to mix. Using the reserved juice, top up the mixture to 600ml/1pint. Use this mixture to make the ice cream following the instructions of your ice cream maker

Blending the pineapple cubes.

Kiwi Ice Cream

Heat the sugar in a saucepan with 150ml/ ¼ pt of water, stirring from time to time until the sugar has dissolved. Bring to the boil and cook for 3 minutes. Remove from the heat and set to one side to cool. Peel the kiwis and roughly chop the flesh. Place them in a blender or food processor with the liquid glycerine and blend until smooth. Add the cooled syrup and double cream, and mix. Use this mixture to make the ice cream following the instructions of your ice cream maker.

Ingredients

125g/4oz granulated sugar
450g/1lb kiwi fruit
    (approx 6)
1 tablespoon liquid glucose
150ml/ ¼ pt double cream

Peeling and chopping the kiwis.

Adding the cream to the blender.

Gooseberry & Elderflower

Place the gooseberries and sugar in a saucepan with 50ml/4tbsp of water. Bring gently to the boil, then reduce the heat to a simmer and cook for 10 minutes or until the gooseberries are tender. Allow to cool then purée in a blender or food processor. Add the cream and elderflower cordial and mix thoroughly. Use this mixture to make the ice cream following the instructions of your ice cream maker

Ingredients

375g/13oz fresh
   gooseberries
75g/3oz caster sugar
300ml/ ½ pt double cream
4 tablespoons elderflower
   cordial

Cooking the gooseberries until soft.

Adding the cordial to the blender.

Raspberry Ice Cream

Heat the sugar with 100ml/ 3½ fl oz of water in a large saucepan, stirring from time to time until the sugar has fully dissolved. Bring to the boil and boil rapidly for 2 minutes then reduce to a simmer and add the raspberries. Continue to cook for 2–3 minutes until the raspberries have collapsed. Remove from the heat and set to one side to cool. Once cooled, add the double cream and stir to mix. Use this mixture to make the ice cream following the instructions of your ice cream maker.

Ingredients
100g/4oz granulated sugar
300g/10 1/2oz raspberries
300ml/ ½ pt double cream

Cooking the raspberries until soft.

Adding the double cream to the pan.

Apricot Ice Cream

Empty the canned apricots into a saucepan and add the ready-to-eat dried apricots. Cover and cook gently until the apricots are soft and cooked through, approximately 15–20 minutes. Leave to cool then purée in a blender or food processor.

In a mixing bowl whisk the egg yolks and sugar until pale and mousse-like. Gently heat the milk and cream in a saucepan until almost boiling, then pour in a steady stream over the sugar and yolks, whisking as you do so. Return the mixture to the pan and cook, stirring all the time

Ingredients

400g/14 oz can apricots in juice
150g/5oz ready-to-eat dried apricots
4 egg yolks
75g/3oz caster sugar
150ml/ ¼ pt double cream
150ml/ ¼ pt milk

Cooling before blending.

until the mixture thickens. You can check the consistency by dipping a wooden spoon into the mixture then running your finger over the back of the spoon. If your finger leaves a clean trail then the mixture is ready.

Remove from the heat and set to one side to cool. Once fully cooled, add the puréed apricots and mix. Use this custard to make the ice cream according to the instructions of your ice cream maker.

Combining the egg yolk and sugar mixture with the milk mixture.

Plum

Empty the plums into a blender or food processor, checking that they have had their stones removed. Blend to a smooth purée then set to one side. In a mixing bowl, whisk the egg yolks and sugar until pale and mousse-like. Gently heat the milk and cream in a saucepan until almost boiling, then pour in a steady stream over the sugar and yolks, whisking as you do so. Return the mixture to the pan and cook, stirring all the time until the mixture thickens. You can check the

Ingredients

570g/ 1¼lb-can plums in
   syrup
2 egg yolks
25g/1oz caster sugar
150ml/ ¼ pt milk
150ml/ ¼ pt double cream

Whisking the egg yolks and sugar.

consistency by dipping a wooden spoon into the mixture then running your finger over the back of the spoon. If your finger leaves a clean trail then the mixture is ready. Remove from the heat and add the plum purée, mixing until fully incorporated. Leave until fully cooled then use this mixture to make the ice cream according to the instructions of your ice cream maker.

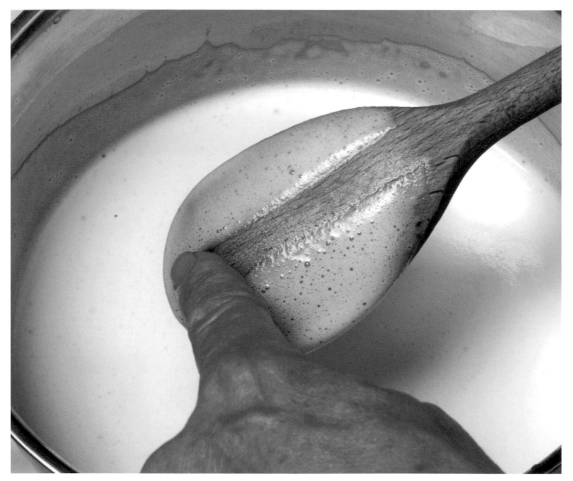

Checking the consistency of the custard.

Peaches & Cream

Heating the peaches and sugar.

Ingredients
400g/14-oz can peaches in
  light syrup
40g/1 ½ oz caster sugar
150ml/ ¼ pt double cream

In a pan heat the peaches and their
syrup with the sugar, stirring from
time to time, until the sugar has
dissolved. Remove from the heat
and set to one side to cool. Once
fully cooled, blend the peaches and
the juice to a purée in a food
processor or blender. Stir in the
cream then use this mixture to make
the ice cream according to the
instructions of your ice cream maker.

Blending the peaches to a purée.

Pear & Ginger

Purée the pears and their syrup in a food processor or blender. Using a sharp knife, chop the stem ginger finely and add to the puréed pears along with the stem ginger syrup. Stir well to mix. Add the cream and stir again. Use this mixture to make the ice cream according to the instructions of your machine.

Ingredients

410g/14-oz can pears in light syrup
2 pieces of preserved stem ginger
2 tablespoons stem ginger syrup
150ml/ ¼ pt double cream

Puréeing the pears in a blender.

Adding the ginger syrup to the pear mix.

4 Fruit Ice Cream

Ingredients

200g/7oz sugar

250ml/9fl oz milk

250ml/9fl oz double cream

1 banana, mashed

1 orange, zested & juiced

1 lemon, zested & juiced

150g/5oz strawberries,
   mashed

Mashed banana mix.

Heat the sugar and milk together, stirring until the sugar has dissolved. Remove from the heat and leave to cool. Once cooled stir in the double cream. Mash the banana with the juiced and zested orange and lemon. Stir into the cream mixture with the mashed strawberries. Use this mixture to make the ice cream following the instructions of your ice cream maker.

Stirring the cream into the strawberries.

NUTTY

Creamy Yoghurt & Hazelnut

Ingredients

150ml/ ¼ pt milk

225g/8oz condensed milk

500g/1lb 2oz Greek
yoghurt

50g/2oz hazelnuts roasted
and chopped

Heating the two milks in a saucepan.

Place the milk and condensed milk in a saucepan and bring gently to just below boiling point, then remove from the heat and put to one side to cool fully. Once cool, add the yoghurt and mix well to combine. Now add the chopped roasted hazelnuts and stir. Following the instructions of your ice cream maker, use the mixture to make your ice cream.

Adding the chopped hazelnuts.

Greek Yoghurt, Honey & Toasted Almond

Heat the oven to 190°C/375°F/Gas mark 5. Place the almonds on a baking tray in a single layer and cook them for approximately 8–10 minutes. Remove from the oven and shake the tray to turn them and check their colour – they should be a rich golden brown. If they need a little longer, return them to the oven but remember to check them regularly, as they will quickly go from not quite cooked to burnt! Remove from the oven and allow to cool for 5–10 minutes, then roughly chop. Set to one side to cool fully. In a large bowl mix together the yoghurt, milk and honey. Then add the cooled nuts and mix. Following the instructions of your ice cream maker, use the mixture to make the ice cream.

Toasting the almonds.

Ingredients
100g/4oz almonds
450g/1lb Greek yoghurt
150ml/ ¼ pt long life full-
   cream milk
100g/4oz honey

Mixing the yoghurt, milk and honey.

Almond Praline

For the praline, place the granulated sugar in a saucepan with 150ml/ ¼ pt of water and heat gently, stirring until the sugar has dissolved. Increase the heat and boil until the mixture becomes a golden caramel, being very careful as boiling sugar is extremely hot! As soon as you reach the golden caramel stage remove the pan from the heat and add the almonds stirring quickly. Then turn the almonds out on to a piece of baking parchment or a greased tin (if the caramel stiffens at this point return it briefly to the heat until it

Ingredients

125g/4 ½ oz granulated sugar

100g/4oz toasted almonds

4 egg yolks

125g/4 ½ oz caster sugar

150ml/ ¼ pt double cream

150ml/ ¼ pt milk

200ml/7fl oz Greek yoghurt

1 teaspoon vanilla essence

Turning out the almonds.

loosens. If, however, the mixture looks granulated it means that the sugar wasn't fully dissolved when you started boiling, so you must start again). Leave to cool, then crush to a coarse powder.

Whisk the egg yolks and sugar in a mixing bowl until pale and mousse-like. In a saucepan, gently heat the milk and cream until almost boiling then pour in a steady stream over the sugar and yolks, whisking as you do so. Return the mixture to the pan and cook, stirring all the time until the mixture thickens. You can check the consistency by dipping a wooden spoon into the mixture then running your finger over the back of the spoon. If your finger leaves a clean trail then the mixture is ready. Remove from the heat and stir in the Greek yoghurt and vanilla essence. Set to one side to cool. Once fully cooled, use this custard to make the ice cream according to the instructions of your ice cream maker. When the ice cream is almost ready add the crushed praline and continue to churn until well mixed.

Whisking the egg yolks and sugar.

Rocky Road

Ingredients

100g/4oz pecan nuts

100g/4oz dark chocolate

100g/4oz mini
   marshmallows

100g/4oz milk chocolate

3 egg yolks

50g/2oz caster sugar

150ml/¼ pt milk

450ml/¾ pt single cream

Preheat the oven to 190°C/375°F/Gas mark 5. Lightly toast the pecans in the oven for 10–12 minutes. Remove from the heat, leave to cool, then chop roughly. Roughly chop the dark chocolate and place in a bowl set over a pan of barely simmering water, ensuring that the bowl is not touching the water. Stir until the chocolate has melted then remove from the heat and pour the chocolate on to a lightly greased baking tray and leave to cool and harden. Once cool break into bite size chunks and mix with the nuts and marshmallows.

Chopping the cooled pecans.

89

Whisk the egg yolks and sugar in a mixing bowl until pale and mousse-like. In a saucepan gently heat the milk and cream until almost boiling then pour in a steady stream over the sugar and yolks, whisking as you do so. Return the mixture to the pan and cook, stirring all the time until the mixture thickens. You can check the consistency by dipping a wooden spoon into the mixture then running your finger over the back of the spoon. If your finger leaves a clean trail then the mixture is ready. Remove from the heat and leave to cool fully. When cold add the nuts, chocolate and marshmallows. Use this mixture to make the ice cream according to your machine instructions.

Breaking the chocolate into bite-size chunks.

Banana Peanut Butter

In a large bowl whisk the egg yolks and caster sugar together until thick and mousse-like. Gently heat the milk and cream until almost boiling then pour in a steady stream over the sugar and yolks, whisking as you do so. Return the mixture to the pan and cook, stirring all the time until the mixture thickens. You can check the consistency by dipping a wooden spoon into the mixture then running your finger over the back of the spoon. If your finger leaves a clean trail then the mixture is ready. Leave to cool fully. Mash the bananas in a bowl until smooth, stir in the peanut butter and add to the cooled custard. Following the instructions of your ice cream maker, use the mixture to make the ice cream.

Ingredients

6 egg yolks

50g/2oz caster sugar

300ml/ ½ pt milk

200ml/7fl oz double cream

1 large ripe banana

3 tablespoons crunchy
   peanut butter

Whisking the egg yolks and sugar.

Adding the peanut butter to the mashed banana.

Maple Pecan

Toasting the pecans.

Spread the pecan nuts on a large baking tray and toast in a moderately hot oven for approximately 10 minutes, or until they smell lightly toasted (if you feel they need a little longer watch them carefully as they will quickly burn). Remove from the oven and when cool enough to handle, roughly chop, then set to one side to cool fully. Whisk the egg yolks and sugar in a mixing bowl until pale and mousse-like. In a saucepan, gently heat the milk until almost boiling then pour in a steady stream over the sugar and yolks, whisking as you do so. Return the mixture to the pan and cook, stirring all the time until the mixture thickens. You can check the consistency by dipping a wooden spoon into the mixture then running your finger over the back of the spoon. If your finger leaves a clean trail then the mixture is ready. Remove from the heat. Add the maple syrup and cream, stirring well to mix. Set to one side to cool fully. Use this mixture to make the ice cream following the instructions of your ice cream maker.

Approximately 2–3 minutes before the ice cream has finished churning, add the chopped nuts.

Ingredients

150g/5oz pecan nuts
2 egg yolks
50g/2oz soft brown sugar
200ml/7fl oz milk
175ml/6fl oz maple syrup
300ml/ ½ pt double cream

Adding chopped nuts during churning.

Honey, Orange & Almond

In a saucepan, heat the sugar and honey with 2 tablespoons water until the sugar has dissolved, then boil for 2 minutes. Add the zest and almonds then cool fully. Stir the crème fraiche and yoghurt together then add the honey and chopped nuts mixture, stirring well to mix. Use this mixture to make the ice cream, following the instructions of your ice cream maker.

Ingredients

75g/3oz granulated sugar
75g/3oz honey
Finely grated zest of 1
    orange
75g/3oz toasted almonds
300ml/ ½ pt crème fraiche
400ml/14fl oz Greek
    yoghurt

Adding the orange zest and almonds to the pan.

Stirring the yoghurt mix into the chopped nuts.

Vanilla Chocolate Almond

Ingredients

50g/2oz dark chocolate

75g/3oz toasted almonds

4 egg yolks

125g/4 ½ oz caster sugar

250ml/9fl oz double cream

250ml/9fl oz whole milk

2 teaspoons vanilla essence

Turning the chocolate almonds out on to a baking tray.

Checking the consistency of the custard.

Chop the chocolate and place in a heat-proof bowl over a pan of simmering water, ensuring that the bottom of the bowl is not touching the water. Stir until the chocolate has melted then add the almonds. Stir the almonds well to coat them in chocolate, then turn them out on to baking parchment or a greased tin. Leave them to cool then chop roughly.

Whisk the egg yolks and sugar in a mixing bowl until pale and mousse-like. In a saucepan gently heat the milk and cream until almost boiling, then pour in a steady stream over the sugar and yolks, whisking as you do so. Return the mixture to the pan and cook, stirring all the time until the mixture thickens. You can check the consistency by dipping a wooden spoon into the mixture then running your finger over the back of the spoon. If your finger leaves a clean trail then the mixture is ready. Remove from the heat and stir in the vanilla essence. Set to one side to cool. Once fully cooled, use this custard to make the ice cream according to the instructions of your ice cream maker. When the ice cream is almost ready, add the chopped chocolate almonds.

Créme de Marron

Mix the créme de marron and cream together. Add the remaining ingredients and mix. Then use this mixture to make the ice cream according to the instructions of your ice cream maker.

Ingredients

250g/9oz créme de marron

250ml/9fl oz double cream

1 teaspoon vanilla essence

2 tablespoons brandy

Mixing the créme marron in with the cream.

Combining the remaining ingredients.

101

Walnut Syrup & Lemon

Grating the lemon zest.

Preheat the oven to 190°C/375°F/Gas mark 5. Spread the walnuts in a single layer on a baking tray and cook for 8–10 minutes or until lightly toasted and golden. Remove from the oven and leave to cool. Beat the egg yolks and syrup together. Add the lemon zest to the egg and syrup mixture. Gently heat the cream and milk together until almost boiling, then pour in a steady stream over the syrup, zest and yolks, whisking as you do so. Return the mixture to the pan and cook stirring all the time until the mixture thickens. You can check the consistency by dipping a wooden spoon into the mixture then running your finger over the back of the spoon. If your finger leaves a clean trail then the mixture is ready. Remove from the heat and leave to cool fully. Once cold stir in the walnuts. Use this mixture to make the ice cream following the instructions of your ice cream maker.

Ingredients

100g/4oz walnuts, roughly chopped

3 egg yolks

75g/3oz golden syrup

Zest of 1 lemon

450ml/¼ pt double cream

300ml/½ pt whole milk

Stirring in the walnuts.

102

Peanut Brittle

Whisking the egg yolks and honey together.

In a mixing bowl, whisk the egg yolks and honey together. Gently heat the cream and milk together until almost boiling, then pour in a steady stream over the yolks and honey, whisking as you do so. Return the mixture to the pan and cook, stirring all the time until the mixture thickens. You can check the consistency by dipping a wooden spoon into the mixture then running your finger over the back of the spoon. If your finger leaves a clean trail then the mixture is ready. Remove from the heat and leave to cool fully. Once cold, use this mixture to make the ice cream following the instructions of your ice cream maker. As you remove the ice cream from the ice cream maker add the crushed peanut brittle and stir once or twice to give a rippled effect. If you over-stir at this point, don't worry – it will just mean that the peanut brittle is not in such distinctive ripples and is more evenly distributed.

Ingredients

4 egg yolks

75g/3oz runny honey

300ml/ ½pt double cream

300ml/ ½pt milk

150g/5oz peanut brittle, roughly crushed

Pouring the cream and milk mixture over the egg yolk mix.

105

Pistachio Ice Cream

In a mixing bowl, whisk the egg yolks and 50g/2oz of the sugar together. Gently heat the creams together until almost boiling. In a food processor or blender, finely chop half the pistachios with the remaining sugar. Stir all the pistachios into the creams. Return the pan to the heat for 2 minutes then pour in a steady stream over the yolks and sugar, whisking as you do so. Return the mixture to the pan and cook, stirring all the time until the mixture thickens. You can check the consistency by dipping a wooden spoon into the mixture then running your finger over the back of the spoon. If your finger leaves a clean trail then the mixture is ready. Remove from the heat and leave to cool. Once cold, use this mixture to make the ice cream following the instructions of your ice cream maker.

Whisking the egg yolks and sugar together.

Ingredients

3 egg yolks
75g/3oz caster sugar
300ml/ ½ pt single cream
300ml/ ½ pt double cream
100g/4oz pistachios,
   roughly chopped

Adding the pistachios to the pan.

106

EXTRA SWEET

Chocolate

Whisking the egg yolks and sugar together.

mixture is ready. Remove from the heat and add the chopped chocolate. Stir until the chocolate is melted and fully incorporated. Leave until fully cooled then use this mixture to make the ice cream according to the instructions of your ice cream maker.

Ingredients

100g/4oz milk chocolate

4 egg yolks

50g/2oz caster sugar

150ml/ ½ pt milk

300ml/ ¼ pt double cream

Finely chop the chocolate and set to one side. In a mixing bowl, whisk the egg yolks and sugar until pale and mousse-like. In a saucepan, gently heat the milk and cream until almost boiling then pour in a steady stream over the sugar and yolks, whisking as you do so. Return the mixture to the pan and cook, stirring all the time until the mixture thickens. You can check the consistency by dipping a wooden spoon into the mixture then running your finger over the back of the spoon. If your finger leaves a clean trail then the

Checking the thickness of the custard.

Toffee Buttermilk

Place the egg yolks and sugar in a large mixing bowl and whisk until the mixture becomes mousse-like. This will take approximately 5–8 minutes. Now pour the milk into a saucepan and place over a gentle heat. Bring almost to the boil then remove from the heat and pour in a steady stream over the egg yolk and sugar mixture, whisking all the time. Return the mixture to the pan and cook over a gentle heat stirring all the time with a wooden spoon until it thickens slightly. You can check the consistency by dipping a wooden spoon into the mixture then running your finger over the back of the spoon. If your finger leaves a clean trail then the mixture is ready. Leave to cool fully, then stir in the buttermilk. Following the instructions of your ice cream maker, use the mixture to make the ice cream.

Whisking the egg yolks and sugar together.

Ingredients

4 egg yolks

175g/6oz dark soft brown
   sugar

600ml/1pt milk

284ml/9 ½ fl oz buttermilk

Checking the consistency of the custard.

Banana Toffee Ice Cream

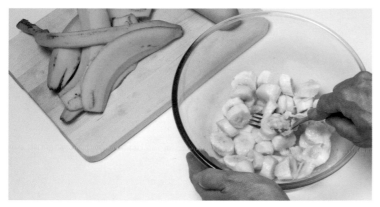

Ingredients

3 ripe bananas

½ lemon, juiced

10 tablespoons dulce de
leche (see note*)

150ml/ ¼ pt fromage frais.

Mashing the bananas.

Mash the bananas thoroughly with the lemon juice. Mix in the Dulce de Leche and fromage frais, stirring well. Following the instructions of your ice cream maker, use this mixture to make the ice cream.

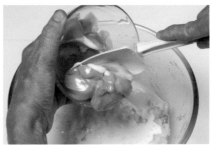

Mixing the dulce de leche and the fromage frais.

*Dulce de leche is a deliciously creamy caramel spread originating from Argentina. It can be found in specialist shops and delicatessens. However, you can make your own quite acceptable alternative. Take an unopened can of condensed milk and place in a large saucepan full of water. Bring to the boil, then reduce the heat to a simmer and cover with a well-fitting lid. Cook for 1 hour 15 minutes, checking regularly that the can is covered by the water. If you need to top up the water always add boiling water or you will slow down the cooking process. DO NOT ALLOW THE PAN TO BOIL DRY AS THE CAN COULD EXPLODE. Once the cooking time is up, remove from the heat and allow to cool fully before opening the can. Remove the contents of the can to a clean, airtight container and store in the fridge. Use as required. It is delicious on toast, as a cake filling, in pancakes and, of course, in ice cream.

Caramel Pineapple

Peel and slice the pineapple lengthways into quarters, removing the hard core. Cut the quarters lengthways once more so you have 8 long pieces. Preheat the grill and line the grill pan with tin foil. Lay the pineapple pieces tightly side by side on the tin foil. Sprinkle the brown sugar over the pineapple and cook until the pineapple is hot and the sugar has caramelised. Set to one side to cool. When cold, purée in a liquidiser or food processor until smooth. In a large bowl, whisk the caster sugar, vanilla essence and egg yolks together until thick and mousse-like. Gently heat the milk and cream until almost boiling, then pour in a steady

Ingredients

1 medium-sized sweet
   pineapple
75g/3oz soft brown sugar
25g/1oz caster sugar
1 teaspoon vanilla essence
3 egg yolks
125ml/4fl oz milk
125ml/4fl oz single cream

Preparing the pineapple.

stream over the sugar and yolks, whisking as you do so. Return the mixture to the pan and cook, stirring all the time until the mixture thickens. You can check the consistency by dipping a wooden spoon into the mixture then running your finger over the back of the spoon. If your finger leaves a clean trail then the mixture is ready. Leave to cool fully, then mix the pineapple purée with the custard and use the mixture to make the ice cream according to the instructions of your machine.

Baking the pineapple and sugar
until caramelised.

Dark Chocolate & Cardamom

Split the cardamom pods and remove the seeds. Crush the seeds with a pestle and mortar and place them in a small bowl. Heat the milk until almost boiling then pour over the cardamom seeds and set to one side to infuse. Once the milk is cool, strain through a fine mesh sieve, reserving the milk and discarding the cardamom seeds. Sift the cocoa into a bowl and add a little of the milk to form a paste then add the rest of the milk, stirring well to blend. Chop the chocolate. In a mixing bowl whisk the egg yolks and sugar until pale and mousse-like. In a saucepan, gently heat the milk and creams until almost boiling then pour in a steady stream over the sugar and yolks, whisking as you do so.

Ingredients

2 cardamom pods

150ml/ ¼ pt milk

1 tablespoon cocoa powder

100g/4oz dark chocolate

4 egg yolks

125g/4 ½ oz granulated
  sugar

300ml/ ½ pt double cream

150ml/ ¼ pt single cream

Crushing the cardamom seeds.

119

Return the mixture to the pan and cook, stirring all the time until the mixture thickens. You can check the consistency by dipping a wooden spoon into the mixture then running your finger over the back of the spoon. If your finger leaves a clean trail then the mixture is ready. Add the chopped chocolate and stir until melted. Set to one side to cool fully. Use this mixture to make the ice cream following the instructions of your ice cream maker.

Adding the chopped chocolate to the pan

White Chocolate

Melting the chocolate over a low heat.

Ingredients

250g/9oz white chocolate

250ml/9fl oz milk

250g/9oz mascarpone

Break the chocolate into small pieces and place in a pan with the milk. Cook over a gentle heat, stirring all the time. Once the chocolate is completely melted, remove from the heat and leave to cool fully. In a large mixing bowl, beat the mascarpone then add a little of the chocolate milk mixture and beat again. Continue doing this until all the chocolate milk has been added. Following the instructions of your ice cream maker, use the mixture to make the ice cream.

Serving suggestion: sandwich the ice cream between biscuits then return to the freezer until ready to serve, or eat straight away.

Adding the chocolate milk mixture to the marscapone.

White Chocolate & Banana

Heating the chocolate until melted.

Ingredients

400g/14oz white chocolate

300ml/ ½ pt milk

2 ripe bananas

1 tablespoon lemon juice

200g/7oz mascarpone

Chop the chocolate. In a saucepan heat the milk until almost boiling then remove from the heat and add the chocolate. Stir until the chocolate has melted. Set to one side to cool fully. Once the mixture is cold, mash the bananas with the lemon juice then add to the mascarpone, stirring to ensure there are no lumps. Finally add the chocolate mixture, stirring well to mix. Use this mixture to make the ice cream, following the instructions of your ice cream maker.

Mashing the bananas with the lemon juice.

Chocolate Orange

Finely chop the chocolate and set to one side. In a mixing bowl whisk the egg yolks and sugar until pale and mousse-like. Gently heat the milk and cream in a saucepan until almost boiling then pour in a steady stream over the sugar and yolks, whisking as you do so. Return the mixture to the pan and cook, stirring all the time, until the mixture thickens. You can check the consistency by dipping a wooden spoon into the mixture then running your finger over the back of the spoon. If your finger leaves a clean trail then the mixture is ready. Remove from the heat, add the chopped chocolate and stir until fully melted. Leave until cool. Stir in the orange zest and then use this mixture to make the ice cream according to the instructions of your ice cream maker.

Heating the cream in a saucepan.

Ingredients

150g/5oz dark chocolate

6 egg yolks

75g/3oz caster sugar

200ml/7fl oz whole milk

300ml/ ½ pt double cream

Finely grated zest of 1
   orange

Zesting the orange

White Chocolate & Dark Chocolate Chunk

Roughly chop the white chocolate and place in a saucepan with the milk. Cook over a gentle heat, stirring all the time, until the chocolate is melted and fully incorporated into the milk. Remove from the heat and allow to cool for 5 minutes, then stir in the double cream and glucose. Leave to cool. Once cold use this mixture to make the ice cream following the instructions of your machine. When the ice cream is almost fully churned add the chocolate chunks and continue to churn until the pieces are fully incorporated and the ice cream is ready.

Melting the chocolate in a saucepan.

Ingredients

200g/7oz white chocolate
200ml/7fl oz milk
300ml/ ½ pt double cream
1 tablespoon liquid glucose
75g/3oz dark chocolate
    chunks

Adding chocolate chunks during the churning process.

Banoffee

In a mixing bowl, whisk the egg yolks and dulce de lait together until fully incorporated and no lumps remain. Gently heat the milk and cream in a saucepan until almost boiling, then pour in a steady stream over the dulce de lait and yolks, whisking as you do so. Return the mixture to the pan and cook, stirring all the time, until the mixture thickens. You can check the consistency by dipping a wooden spoon into the mixture then running your finger over the back of the spoon. If your finger leaves a clean trail then the mixture is ready. Remove from the heat and leave until fully cooled. Stir in the banana and vanilla essence. Use this mixture to make the ice cream according to the instructions of your ice cream maker.

Ingredients

4 egg yolks
125g/4oz dulce de lait
250ml/9fl oz milk
250ml/9fl oz double cream
1 large ripe banana
1 teaspoon vanilla essence

Whisking the egg yolks and dulce de lait together.

Adding the mashed banana to the pan.

Caramel Honey Chocolate Chunk

Ingredients
75g/3oz granulated sugar

50g/2oz honey

250ml/9fl oz milk

250ml/9fl oz double cream

75g/3oz dark chocolate
  chunks

Adding the honey to the pan.

In a small saucepan, heat the sugar with 100ml/3 1/2fl oz water, stirring from time to time until the sugar has dissolved. Increase the heat to a rolling boil and cook without stirring until the sugar starts to caramelise, then remove from the heat and add the honey, stirring to mix. Stir in the milk and cream and leave to cool fully. Use this mixture to make the ice cream according to the instructions of your ice cream maker. Add the chocolate chunks 5 minutes before the ice cream has finished churning.

Adding chocolate chunks during churning.

Chocolate mint

In a saucepan, gently heat the milk, cream and mint sprigs until almost boiling. Remove from the heat and set to one side. Finely chop the chocolate and set to one side. Remove the mint sprigs from the milk and discard. Gently heat the infused milk and cream until hot but not boiling. In a mixing bowl, whisk the egg yolks and sugar until pale and mousse-like. Pour in a steady stream over the sugar and yolks, whisking as you do so. Return the mixture to the pan and cook, stirring all the time, until the mixture thickens. You can check the consistency by dipping a wooden spoon into

Ingredients

300ml/ ½ pt milk

450ml/ ¾ pt double cream

2 sprigs of fresh mint

100g/4oz dark chocolate

4 egg yolks

75g/3oz caster sugar

Infusing the milk and cream with mint.

the mixture then running your finger over the back of the spoon. If your finger leaves a clean trail then the mixture is ready. Remove from the heat and add the chopped chocolate. Stir until the chocolate is melted and fully incorporated. Leave until fully cooled, then make the ice cream according to the instructions of your ice cream maker.

Stirring until the chocolate is fully incorporated.

Triple Chocolate Ice Cream

In a mixing bowl, whisk the egg yolks and sugar together. Gently heat the creams together until almost boiling then pour in a steady stream over the yolks and sugar, whisking as you do so. Return the mixture to the pan and cook, stirring all the time until the mixture thickens. You can check the consistency by dipping a wooden spoon into the mixture then running your finger over the back of the spoon. If your finger leaves a clean trail then the mixture is ready. Remove from the heat and divide equally between three bowls. Add the chopped dark chocolate to one bowl and stir until the chocolate is

Ingredients

4 egg yolks

75g/3oz caster sugar

300ml/ ½ pt double cream

450ml/ ¾ pt single cream

300ml/ ½ pt whole milk

50g/2oz dark chocolate,
   chopped

Dividing the mixture between three bowls.

fully melted and incorporated.
Repeat this process with the other
bowls and the milk and white
chocolate. Leave to cool. Once the
chocolate mixtures are cold, use the
dark chocolate mixture first to make
ice cream in your machine. Once the
ice cream is fully churned turn it out
into a loaf tin that is lined with cling
film. Level the surface and store in
the freezer while you make the two
remaining ice creams. Repeat the
process with the milk chocolate
mixture and the white chocolate,
building three layers of ice cream in
the loaf tin. To serve, turn out on to a
serving plate, remove the cling film
and cut into slices.

Building the ice cream layers in the loaf tin.

White Chocolate & Ginger Cake

Place the crushed biscuits in a bowl and add the melted butter, stirring well to mix. Tip the mixture into a 23cm/9in loose-bottomed flan tin with deep sides. Press the mixture into the base levelling it with the back of a spoon. Chill in the fridge until ready to use.

Heat the milk and the chocolate together, stirring until the chocolate has melted and is completely incorporated. In a mixing bowl, whisk the egg yolks and sugar together. Gently heat the cream until almost boiling then pour in a steady stream over the yolks and sugar, whisking as you do so. Return the mixture to the pan and cook, stirring all the time, until the mixture thickens. You can check the consistency by dipping a wooden spoon into the mixture then running your finger over the back of the spoon. If your finger leaves a clean trail then the mixture is ready. Remove from the heat and stir in the

Making the biscuit base.

milk and chocolate mixture, then set to one side to cool. Once the mixture is cold, whisk the egg white in a clean mixing bowl until it forms soft peaks then gently fold into the cooled chocolate mixture. Use this mixture to make the ice cream following the instructions of your ice cream maker. Once the ice cream is ready, spread it over the biscuit base, levelling the surface. Store in the freezer until ready to serve. Dust the surface with cocoa powder before serving if desired.

Ingredients

225g/8oz ginger biscuits, crushed
75g/3oz butter, melted
175g/6oz white chocolate, chopped
300ml/ ½ pt whole milk
2 egg yolks
50g/2oz caster sugar
300ml/ ½ pt single cream
1 egg white

Whisking the egg whites to soft-peak stage.

141

Buffalo & Brown Sugar

Heating the sugar and water in a pan.

Ingredients

125g/4 ½ oz dark
   muscovado sugar
6 egg yolks
500ml/1pt buffalo yoghurt

Heat the sugar in a saucepan with 150ml/1/4pt of water, stirring from time to time. Once the sugar has dissolved bring the syrup to a rolling boil and cook until the mixture reaches 110°C/225°F on a sugar thermometer. Remove from the heat and allow to cool for 5 minutes. Place the egg yolks in a mixing bowl then pour the syrup in a thin steady stream on to the yolks, whisking all the time. Continue whisking until the mixture becomes thick and mousse-like. Fold in the yoghurt and when the mixture is cool use it to make the ice cream following the instructions on your machine.

Folding in the yoghurt.

Caramallow Ice Cream

Adding the milk to the marshmallows and caramel.

Ingredients

150g/5oz marshmallows

100g/4oz caramels

450ml/ ¾ pt milk

300ml/ ½ pt double cream

Place the marshmallows, caramels and milk in a saucepan over a gentle heat, stirring until the caramels and marshmallows are completely melted and the mixture is fully combined. Set to one side to cool. Once cooled stir in the cream and then use this mixture to make the ice cream following the instructions of your ice cream maker.

Stirring until all ingredients are fully combined.

DELICIOUS BUT DIFFERENT

Christmas Pudding Ice Cream

Pouring brandy over the dried fruit.

Adding the brandy-soaked fruits during churning.

Ingredients

75g/3oz glacé cherries, roughly chopped

50g/2oz crystallised ginger, chopped

50g/2oz candied peel, chopped

100g/4oz sultanas

3 tablespoons brandy

3 egg yolks

75g/3oz granulated sugar

300ml/ ½ pt double cream

150ml/ ¼ pt milk

1 teaspoon ground mixed spice

50g/2oz toasted almonds, roughly chopped

Mix the cherries, ginger, candied peel and sultanas in a bowl, then pour the brandy over the fruits and set to one side for 2–3 hours to soak, stirring occasionally. Whisk the egg yolks and sugar in a mixing bowl until pale and mousse-like. In a saucepan gently heat the cream, milk and mixed spice until almost boiling, then pour in a steady stream over the sugar and yolks, whisking as you do so. Return the mixture to the pan and cook, stirring all the time until the mixture thickens. You can check the consistency by dipping a wooden spoon into the mixture then running your finger over the back of the spoon. If your finger leaves a clean trail then the mixture is ready. Remove from the heat and leave to cool fully. Use this mixture to make the ice cream according to the instructions on your machine, adding the soaked fruits as the machine is churning.

Eton Mess

To make the meringues preheat the oven to 150°C/300°F/Gas mark 2. Whisk the egg white in a bowl until it reaches the stiff peak stage. Add the brown sugar, a tablespoon at a time, whisking well between each addition until all the sugar has been used. Line a baking sheet with baking parchment and place heaped tablespoons of the mixture on to the parchment. Bake in the oven for 1½ hours, then turn off the oven but leave the meringues in the oven to cool.

In a mixing bowl whisk the egg yolks and sugar until pale and mousse-like. Gently heat the milk and cream in a saucepan until almost boiling, then pour in a steady stream over the sugar and yolks, whisking as you do so. Return the mixture to the pan and cook, stirring all the time until the mixture thickens. You can

Ingredients

1 egg white
50g/2oz brown sugar
4 egg yolks
75g/3oz caster sugar
250ml/9fl oz milk
250ml/9fl oz double cream
1 teaspoon vanilla essence
175g/6oz strawberries,
    chopped

Whisking the egg whites to stiff peaks.

151

check the consistency by dipping a wooden spoon into the mixture then running your finger over the back of the spoon. If your finger leaves a clean trail then the mixture is ready. Remove from the heat and stir in the vanilla essence. Set to one side to cool. Once fully cooled use this custard to make the ice cream according to the instructions of your ice cream maker. When the ice cream is almost ready, add the chopped strawberries and the meringues roughly crushed. Continue to churn until the strawberries and meringues are lightly mixed in and the ice cream is ready.

Adding the strawberry and meringue mix.

Brown Bread

Preheat the oven to 190°C/ 375°F/Gas mark 5. In a bowl, mix the breadcrumbs and sugar together, then sprinkle them in a thin layer over a baking sheet lined with parchment paper. Bake for 15–20 minutes until golden and crisp. You may need to stir the outside edges to the middle and vice versa, to prevent burning. Remove from the oven and leave to cool.

Whisk the egg yolks and sugar in a mixing bowl until pale and mousse-like. In a saucepan, gently heat the milk and cream until almost boiling then pour in a steady stream over the sugar and yolks, whisking as you do so. Return the mixture to the pan and cook, stirring all the time until the mixture thickens. You can

Ingredients

75g/3oz wholemeal
    breadcrumbs
125g/41/2oz Demerara
    sugar
4 egg yolks
75g/3oz caster sugar
300ml/1/2pt single cream
300ml/1/2pt milk
1 vanilla pod

Combining the breadcrumbs and sugar.

check the consistency by dipping a wooden spoon into the mixture then running your finger over the back of the spoon. If your finger leaves a clean trail then the mixture is ready. Remove from the heat and allow to cool fully before using this mixture to make the ice cream. When the ice cream is a minute or two away from being ready, add the toasted breadcrumbs.

Baking the breadcrumb mix until brown.

Spiced Banana

Caramelising the sugar.

Slice the bananas into a bowl and add the lemon juice, mix well and set to one side. Place the caster sugar and 250ml/9fl oz water in a large saucepan. Heat and stir gently until the sugar has dissolved. Then increase the heat until the mixture is boiling. Continue to cook without stirring until the mixture turns golden brown and caramelises. Remove from the heat, being very careful as the mixture will be extremely hot. Carefully add 100ml/3½ fl oz hot water, stirring well to mix. Beware – it may spit as you do this. Add the lemon juice and sliced bananas and toss well to mix. Set to one side and allow to cool fully. Heat the milk, star anise and cinnamon in a saucepan over a gentle heat until almost boiling. Then remove from the heat and leave to infuse.

Once both mixtures are fully cooled, purée the banana and caramel mixture then strain the spiced milk through a fine sieve and add to the banana purée. Mix well. Following the instructions of your ice cream maker, use the mixture to make the ice cream.

Ingredients

4 ripe bananas, peeled
1 lemon juiced
175g/6oz caster sugar
250ml/9fl oz milk
5 star anise
1 stick cinnamon

Adding the milk to the spices.

Cream Liqueur Ice Cream

In a mixing bowl, whisk the egg yolks and sugar until pale and mousse-like. Gently heat the cream in a saucepan until almost boiling then pour in a steady stream over the sugar and yolks, whisking as you do so. Return the mixture to the pan and cook, stirring all the time until the mixture thickens. You can check the consistency by dipping a wooden spoon into the mixture then running your finger over the back of the spoon. If your finger leaves a clean trail then the mixture is ready. Remove from the heat and leave to cool fully. When cold, add the cream liqueur. Use this mixture to make the ice cream according to the instructions on your machine.

Ingredients

4 egg yolks

75g/3oz caster sugar

450ml/ ¾ pt single cream

300ml/ ½ pt cream liqueur

Adding the heated cream to the egg yolk and sugar mix.

Adding the cream liqueur.

Caramel with Salted Butter

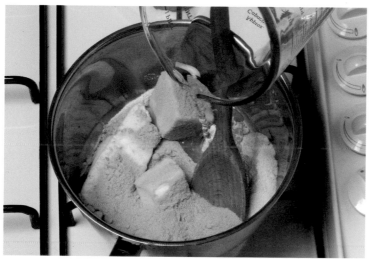

Ingredients

150g/5oz soft brown sugar

100g/4oz salted butter

¼ teaspoon salt

250ml/9fl oz milk

250ml/9fl oz double cream

Placing the sugar, butter and salt in the pan.

Place the sugar, butter and salt in a large saucepan with 90ml/3fl oz cold water. Heat and stir until the butter has melted and the sugar has dissolved. Increase the heat and boil without stirring until the mixture reaches 130°C/250°F on a sugar thermometer. Remove from the heat and carefully add the milk stirring to mix. Allow to cool for 10 minutes then add the cream and mix well. Allow to cool fully then follow the instructions of your ice cream maker to make the ice cream.

Stirring the milk into the caramel mix.

Rum & Vanilla

In a saucepan heat the sugar with 150ml/ ¼ pt water, stirring from time to time. Once the sugar has dissolved, bring the syrup to a rolling boil and cook until the mixture reaches 110°C/225°F on a sugar thermometer. Remove from the heat and allow to cool for 5 minutes. Place the egg yolks in a mixing bowl then pour the syrup in a thin steady stream on to the yolks, whisking all the time. Continue whisking until the mixture becomes thick and mousse-like. Gently fold in the remaining ingredients and when this mixture is cold use it to make the ice cream, following the instructions on your machine.

Heating the sugar and water in the pan.

Ingredients

125g/4 ½ oz caster sugar
6 egg yolks
3 tablespoons dark rum
1 teaspoon vanilla essence
300ml/ ½ pt double cream
150ml/ ¼ pt milk
150ml/ ¼ pt single cream

Pouring the cooled syrup over the eggs.

Chilli Chocolate

Roughly chop the chocolate and place in a saucepan with the milk. Cook over a gentle heat, stirring all the time, until the chocolate is melted and fully incorporated into the milk. Finely chop the chillies (if you like hot flavours keep the seeds, if not discard them). In a mixing bowl whisk the egg yolks and sugar until pale and mousse-like. Gently heat the chillies, cream and milk in a saucepan until almost boiling, then pour in a steady stream over the sugar and yolks, whisking as you do so. Return the mixture to the pan and cook, stirring all the time until the mixture thickens. You can check the consistency by dipping a wooden spoon into the mixture then running your finger over the back of the spoon. If your finger leaves a clean trail then the mixture is ready. Once cold, use this mixture to make the ice cream following the instructions of your ice cream maker.

Ingredients
100g/4oz dark chocolate, preferably 85% cocoa solids

150ml/ ¼ pt milk

2 small red chillies

3 egg yolks

100g/4oz granulated sugar

150ml/1/4 pt single cream

300ml/ ½ pt double cream

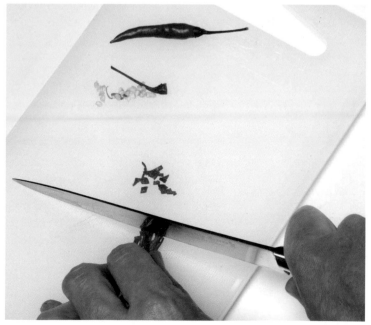

Liquorice

Cut the liquorice into small pieces and place in a pan with 150ml/ ¼ pt of water. Cook over a gentle heat stirring from time to time, until the liquorice is melted. If the mixture becomes too thick, add the milk and continue to cook, stirring until fully mixed. It does not matter if a few pieces of liquorice remain unmelted. Pour into a bowl and add the remaining ingredients, stirring well to mix. Once this mixture is cold use it to make the ice cream following the instructions of your ice cream maker.

Melting the liquorice in a saucepan.

Ingredients
150g/5oz soft liquorice
100ml/3fl oz milk
300ml/ ½ pt double cream
2 tablespoons liquid glucose

Adding the liquid glucose to the mix.

Amaretti & Sherry Ice Cream

Adding the sherry to the cream and sugar mix.

Ingredients

300ml/ ½ pt single cream

50g/2oz caster sugar

150ml/ ¼ pt double cream

4 tablespoons cream sherry

1 egg white

75g/3oz amaretti biscuits,
   lightly crushed

In small saucepan, gently heat the single cream and sugar, stirring from time to time, until the sugar has dissolved. Remove from the heat and leave to cool. Once cold, stir in the double cream and sherry. In a clean bowl whisk the egg white until it stands in soft peaks then fold it into the cream and sherry mixture. Following the instructions of your ice cream maker, use the mixture to make the ice cream, adding the crushed amaretti to the machine approximately 5 minutes before the ice cream has finished churning.

Adding the crushed biscuits during churning.

169

Apple & Brandied Raisin

Leaving the apples to cool.

Ingredients

50g/2oz sultanas

1 tablespoon brandy

450g/1lb cooking apples,
    peeled cored and
    chopped

100g/4oz caster sugar

300ml/ ½ pt single cream

300ml/ ½ pt double cream

Put the sultanas in a bowl along with the brandy, stir and leave to one side to soak. Place the chopped apples, sugar and 100ml/31/2fl oz of water in a saucepan and bring to the boil then reduce the heat to a gentle simmer and continue to cook until the apples are tender and all the liquid has evaporated. Remove from the heat and cool. Once cold, purée the apples in a food processor or blender. Then add the soaked sultanas and creams, stirring well to mix. Use this mixture to make the ice cream following the instructions of your ice cream maker.

Adding the soaked sultanas to the mix.

Deep-fried Ice Cream

Scoop the ice cream on to a baking sheet lined with baking parchment and return to the freezer for 4 hours or preferably overnight. Whisk the egg whites until they form soft peaks. Mix the cornflakes and flaked nuts together. Remove the ice cream from the freezer and, using two forks, dip the scoops in the egg white then roll in the cornflake mixture. Return to the freezer for a further hour. When you are ready to serve the ice cream, heat the oil to 180°C/350°F. Carefully deep-fry each scoop in the hot oil for approximately 25 seconds or until golden and crisp (you may need to do these in batches). Drain on kitchen paper and serve immediately. Good with soft fruits.

Ingredients
8 scoops of your favourite
  ice cream
2 egg whites
125g/4 ½ oz crushed
  cornflakes
50g/2oz flaked almonds
Oil for deep-frying

Whisking the egg whites to soft-peak stage.

Rolling the ice cream scoops in the cornflake mixture.

173

Baked Alaska

Placing an ice cream scoop on a cake disc.

Ingredients

6 ½-in slices of Madeira
    cake

2 egg whites

100g/4oz caster sugar

6 scoops of ice cream of
    your choice

Using a round cookie cutter slightly larger than your ice cream scoops, cut out 6 discs of Madeira cake. Place a scoop of ice cream on each disc of cake and return to the freezer on a baking tray covered with baking parchment or silicone for at least 4 hours or preferably overnight. Approximately 30 minutes before you are ready to serve the baked alaskas, preheat the oven to 220°C/425°F/Gas mark 7. In a mixing bowl, whisk the egg whites until they stand in soft peaks then whisk in the sugar, a spoonful at a time, until the mixture is stiff and glossy and all the sugar has been incorporated. Working quickly, remove the baking tray from the freezer and roughly cover each disc of Madeira cake and ice cream with the meringue mixture, ensuring that each one is completely covered right down to the paper. Place the baking tray in the preheated oven for 6–8 minutes, or until the meringue starts to brown in places. Remove from the oven and serve immediately.

Spooning the meringue mixture over the ice cream.

Smoked Salmon & Dill Ice Cream

Chop the smoked salmon and place in a small pan with the double cream. Heat gently, then remove from the heat and set to one side to infuse. Once cooled add the remaining ingredients and stir to mix. Add salt and freshly ground black pepper to taste. Use this mixture to make the ice cream according to the instructions on your machine.

Ingredients

100g/4oz smoked salmon

300ml/ ½ pt double cream

½ lemon juiced

1 tablespoon liquid glucose

2 tablespoons dill, chopped

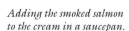

*Adding the smoked salmon
to the cream in a saucepan.*

Pouring in the liquid glucose.

Tomato & Basil

Gently heat the cream with the sprig of basil until almost boiling, then remove from the heat and set to one side to infuse. Once cooled, remove the basil and discard. Add the tomato juice to the cooled cream and add salt and freshly ground black pepper to taste. Stir in the glucose and chopped basil. Taste to check the seasoning and adjust if necessary. Now use this mixture to make the ice cream according to the instructions on your machine. This makes an unusual but tasty starter.

Adding the sprig of basil to the cream.

Ingredients

300ml/ ½ pt double cream

300ml/ ½ pt tomato juice

Large sprig basil plus 2
  teaspoons basil, finely
  chopped

½ teaspoon salt

2 tablespoons liquid glucose

Freshly ground black
  pepper

Pouring the tomato juice into the cooled cream.

178

SORBETS

Bloody Mary Sorbet

Mix the liquids together. Add the cayenne pepper and celery salt and mix well. Then make your sorbet following the instructions on your machine. This is still alcoholic, as freezing does not alter the alcohol content, so be careful who you serve this to! Serve as a starter, or even slightly slushy as a cocktail. If it is not fully frozen at the end of churning, place it in the freezer for half an hour.

Ingredients

400ml/14fl oz tomato juice
60ml/4 tablespoons vodka
1 teaspoon liquid glucose
2 teaspoons lemon juice
¼ teaspoon celery salt
Pinch cayenne pepper

Combining the liquids.

Adding the seasoning.

Pear Sorbet

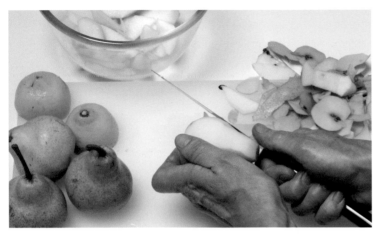

Preparing the fruit.

Ingredients

125g/4 ½ oz granulated
sugar
550g/1lb 3oz ripe pears
1 lemon
3 tablespoons liquid glucose

Place the sugar in a large saucepan with 250ml/9fl oz of cold water. Cook over a gentle heat, stirring from time to time, until the sugar is dissolved. Meanwhile peel and core the pears, then slice thinly into a bowl. Squeeze the juice from the lemon over the pears and toss thoroughly to ensure the pears are coated in the lemon juice. Add the pears and lemon juice to the sugar and water mixture and mix. Bring to the boil then reduce the heat to a gentle simmer for about 10 minutes or until the pears are soft. Stir in the glucose and then remove from the heat and leave to cool. Once cooled, place in a food processor or blender and process until you have a smooth consistency. Following the instructions of your ice cream maker, use the purée to make the sorbet. As it has quite a thick consistency to start with, it may need a shorter time for churning.

Blending the ingredients.

Pink Grapefruit Sorbet

Wash and dry two of the grapefruits then, using a sharp knife, cut thin strips of zest. If you cut off some of the pith as well trim it away and discard it, as it will give an unpleasant bitterness to the flavour. Place the sugar in a large saucepan with 400ml/14fl oz cold water and the strips of zest. Cook over a gentle heat, stirring from time to time until the sugar is dissolved. Remove the strips of zest and discard. Bring to the boil and cook for one minute then remove from the heat and leave to cool fully. Squeeze the juice from the grapefruits and add to the sugar syrup along with the glucose. Stir to mix. Once the mixture is completely cold it is ready to use. Follow the instructions of your ice cream maker to make the sorbet.

Preparing the grapefruit zest.

Ingredients

4 pink grapefruits

200g/7oz sugar

2 tablespoons liquid glucose

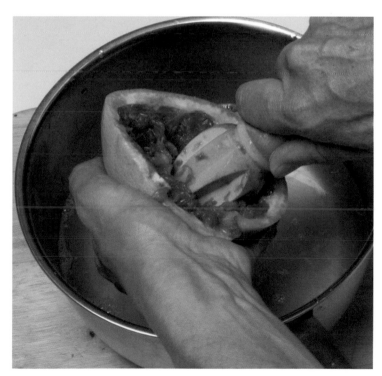

Juicing the grapefruit.

Strawberry Sorbet

Preparing the strawberries.

Ingredients
700g/1 ½ lb strawberries
175g/6oz caster sugar
1 tablespoon liquid glucose

Wash and hull the strawberries, then slice or roughly chop before blending to a purée in a liquidiser or food processor. Place the sugar in a pan with 150ml/ ¼ pt water and heat, gently stirring, until the sugar has dissolved. Remove from the heat and set to one side to cool fully. Combine the strawberries, syrup and glucose and, following the instructions of your ice cream maker, use the mixture to make the sorbet.

Pouring the glucose into the blender.

Strawberry & Mango Sorbet

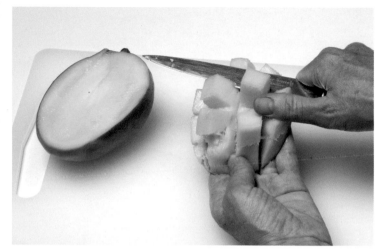

Ingredients

175g/ 6oz caster sugar

1 large ripe mango

300g/10 ½ oz strawberries

1 lemon, juiced

Preparing the mango.

Heat the sugar in a saucepan with 150ml/ ¼ pt water, stirring from time to time until the sugar has dissolved. Remove from the heat and set to one side to cool. Peel the mango and roughly chop the flesh. Roughly chop the strawberries and purée in a food processor or blender. Add the mango, and lemon juice. Blend until smooth. Add the cooled syrup and mix. Use this mixture to make the sorbet following the instructions of your ice cream maker.

Adding the mango to the blender.

Peach Sorbet

Cover the peaches with boiling water and allow to stand for 5 minutes, or until the skins have loosened. Peel the peaches and cut the flesh from the stones, discarding the skins and stones. Place the flesh and sugar in a large saucepan with 100ml/ 3½ fl oz cold water and bring gently to the boil, stirring from time to time, to dissolve the sugar.

Cover the pan with a well-fitting lid and reduce the heat to a gentle simmer. Cook for 10 minutes then remove from the heat and leave to cool. Once cool, purée the mixture in a food processor or blender. Use this mixture to make the sorbet according to the instructions of your ice cream maker.

Ingredients
6 fresh ripe peaches
100g/4oz caster sugar

Preparing the peaches.

Puréeing the cooled mixture.

Mango Sorbet

Dissolve the sugar in 150ml/ ¼ pt cold water, then bring to the boil. Cook at a rolling boil for 3 minutes then remove from the heat and allow to cool. Once cooled, stir the syrup into the mango pulp. Use this mixture to make the sorbet according to the instructions of your ice cream maker.

Ingredients
100g/4oz caster sugar
850g/1lb 4oz mango pulp

Heating the sugar and water in a pan.

Adding the cooled syrup to the mango pulp.

Grapefruit Sorbet

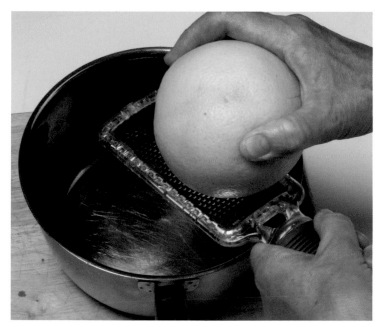

Zesting the grapefruit.

Ingredients

4 large grapefruits

250g/9oz sugar

1 tablespoon liquid glucose

Place the sugar in a large saucepan with 500ml/18fl oz cold water. Cook over a gentle heat, stirring from time to time. Once the sugar has completely dissolved, bring the syrup to the boil and cook for 2 minutes, then remove from the heat. Wash and dry two of the grapefruits, then finely grate the zest and add to the sugar syrup. Squeeze the juice from the grapefruits and add to the sugar syrup along with the glucose. Stir to mix. Once the mixture is completely cold it is ready to use. Following the instructions of your ice cream maker, use the mixture to make the sorbet. This is very refreshing and could even be served as a starter. If you have time, you can serve the sorbet in the

squeezed grapefruit halves. Pull the
squeezed and juiced flesh from
inside the grapefruit, fill with sorbet,
level the tops and serve, or store in
the freezer until ready to serve.

*Preparing the grapefruit for
serving.*

Orange Sorbet with Caramelised Zest

Finely grate the zest of one orange and add to 100g/4oz of the sugar in a saucepan along with 200ml/7fl oz of water. Bring to the boil, stirring from time to time, until the sugar has dissolved. Then boil for 3 minutes before removing from the heat. Strain through a fine sieve, discarding the zest, and set the flavoured syrup to one side to cool. Using a sharp knife remove the peel from another of the oranges, ensuring that it does not include any of the white pith as this will make the mixture bitter. Cut the peel into very fine strips. In a small saucepan

Ingredients
5 juicy oranges
125g/5oz granulated sugar
1 tablespoon liquid glucose

Preparing the orange peel.

199

dissolve the remaining 25g/1oz of sugar in 3 tablespoons of water, then bring to the boil and cook without stirring until the mixture begins to caramelise and turn a light golden brown. Remove from the heat and toss in the thinly shredded zest. Stir quickly then turn out on to a lightly oiled baking sheet and leave to cool. Juice the oranges and stir into the flavoured syrup with the glucose. Use this mixture to make the sorbet according to the instructions on your machine. A minute or two before your sorbet is ready, crumble the caramelised zest into the sorbet and churn to mix.

Caramelising the mixture.

Granny Smith Sorbet

Place the sugar in a large saucepan along with 125ml/4fl oz cold water. Cook over a gentle heat, stirring from time to time, until the sugar has dissolved. Increase the heat until the mixture is boiling. Remove from the heat, stir in the glucose, then leave until completely cool. Wash, quarter and core the apples (do not remove the skins as they give the sorbet its wonderful colour) then juice them. (If you don't have a juicer you can blend them in a food processor or blender, then strain through a fine mesh sieve, pressing down on the pulp to extract as much of the juice as possible.) You need approximately 500ml/1pt of juice. Add the juice to the cooled syrup and stir well to mix. Following the instructions of your ice cream maker use the mixture to make the sorbet.

Dissolving the sugar in the water.

Ingredients

125g/5oz granulated sugar
1 tablespoon liquid glucose
8–10 Granny Smith apples

Extracting the juice from the apples.

203

Raspberry Sorbet

Heat the sugar in a saucepan with 150ml/ ¼ pt of water, stirring until the sugar is fully dissolved. Bring to the boil and cook for a further 3 minutes, then remove from the heat and set to one side to cool. Purée the raspberries in a blender or food processor, then add the lemon juice and glucose. Add the raspberry mixture to the cooled syrup and stir well to mix. Use this mixture to make the sorbet following the instructions of your ice cream maker.

Ingredients

150g/5oz granulated sugar
400g/14oz fresh
    raspberries
1 tablespoon lemon juice
1 tablespoon liquid glucose

Blending the raspberries.

Stirring the puree into the cooled syrup.

Lemon & Ginger Sorbet

Thinly slice the lemon and place in a large saucepan with a well-fitting lid along with the sugar and 500ml/18fl oz water. Bring to the boil then reduce the heat to a gentle simmer and cover with the lid. Cook for 1 hour, then remove from the heat and set to one side to cool fully. Once cold, blend the mixture to a purée in a liquidiser or food processor. Add the stem ginger syrup and mix. You need to have 500ml/18fl oz of mixture in order for the sugar to liquid ratio to provide the right freezing consistency, so pour it into a measuring jug and, if necessary, top it up with cold water. Then, following the instructions of your ice cream maker, use the mixture to make the sorbet.

Leaving the lemon and syrup mix to cool.

Ingredients
1 unwaxed lemon
75g/3oz sugar
6 tablespoons stem ginger
  syrup

Adding the glucose to the mix.

Lemon Sorbet

Wash the lemons, then finely grate the zest from three of them and stir into the sugar. Heat the sugar, zest and 350ml/12fl oz of water in a saucepan, stirring from time to time until the sugar has dissolved. Bring to the boil and boil rapidly for 3 minutes. Remove from the heat and allow to cool. Squeeze the juice from the lemons – you need about 300ml/ ½ pt. Mix the lemon juice and flavoured syrup together and use to make the sorbet following the instructions on your machine.

Ingredients

6 juicy lemons

100g/4oz granulated sugar

Zesting the lemons.

Juicing the lemons.

Lime & Lemon Sorbet

Adding the lime juice to the pan.

Ingredients
6 limes
200g/7oz sugar
2 lemons

Blending the ingredients.

Wash the limes then finely grate the zest from three and set to one side. Juice all six limes and put the juice into a pan with the sugar. Heat gently, stirring from time to time, until the sugar has dissolved. Remove from the heat and add 300ml/ ½ pt of cold water plus the reserved lime zest and the juice of the two lemons. Stir to mix then set to one side to cool. Purée in a food processor, then use to make the sorbet following the instructions on your ice cream maker.

Apricot Sorbet

Empty the two cans of apricots into a large saucepan and bring to the boil. Continue to cook until the syrup has reduced by half. Remove from the heat and leave to cool. Once cooled, purée using a food processor or blender. Use this mixture to make your sorbet following the instructions on your ice cream maker.

Heating the apricots in a pan.

Ingredients

2 x 420g/15-oz cans of
  apricot halves in syrup

Blending the cooled apricots.

Melon Sorbet

Ingredients

100g/4oz sugar

1 ripe Galia melon

Preparing the melon.

Place the sugar in saucepan with 150ml/ $\frac{1}{4}$ pt of water. Bring to the boil, stirring from time to time until the sugar has dissolved. Boil rapidly for 3 minutes, then remove from the heat and leave to cool. Peel and deseed the melon, roughly chop the flesh and place in a food processor or blender and process until you have a purée. Add the cooled syrup and mix. Following the instructions of your ice cream machine, use this mixture to make the sorbet.

Blend the melon to a purée.

Mulled Wine Sorbet

Place all the ingredients in a large saucepan and bring gently to almost boiling point, stirring from time to time. Remove from the heat and leave to cool. Strain and discard the fruits and spices. Following the instructions of your ice cream machine use this mixture to make the sorbet.

Placing the ingredients in a saucepan.

Ingredients

8 cloves

1 stick of cinnamon

450ml/ ¾ pt red wine

150g/5oz granulated sugar

3 thick slices of orange

3 thick slices of lemon

3 tablespoons brandy

Straining the mixture.

Asti & Elderflower Sorbet

Ingredients
1 egg white
150ml/ ¼ pt elderflower
   cordial
450ml/ ¾ pt Asti
   Spumante

*Whisking the egg whites to soft-
peak stage.*

In a mixing bowl, whisk the egg
white until it forms soft peaks.
Gently fold in the elderflower cordial
and the Asti Spumante. This is
easier if you stir in one tablespoon
first, then fold through the
remainder. Following the
instructions of your ice cream
machine use this mixture to make
the sorbet. This is a light, soft-
scooping sorbet.

*Folding the egg whites into the Asti
Spumante.*

219

Nectarine & Framboise Sorbet

Ingredients

600g/1lb 5oz ripe
   nectarines
50g/2oz caster sugar
4 tablespoons Framboise
   liqueur

*Placing the nectarines in a
large saucepan.*

Place the nectarines in a large bowl and cover with boiling water. Leave to stand for 1–2 minutes, then drain. This makes it easy to remove the skins. Once they are skinned, roughly chop the flesh and place in a pan along with any juice that has collected on the chopping board. Add the sugar and 100ml/3 ½ fl oz water. Cook over a gentle heat until the sugar has dissolved, then remove from the heat and set to one side to cool. Once cold, stir in the Framboise liqueur. Use this mixture to make the sorbet following the instructions of your ice cream machine.

Adding the Framboise to the blender.

BISCUITS

Hazelnut Shortbread

Preheat the oven to 170°C/325°F/Gas mark 3. In a food processor or blender grind the hazelnuts in short bursts until they are finely chopped. Beat the butter and sugar together until light and creamy. Add the flour and hazelnuts and mix again to form a stiff dough. On a lightly greased baking tray shape the dough into a 30cm/12in round. This can be done by rolling or simply flattening out the mixture with the heel of your hand, pinching together any cracks that may appear. Sprinkle over the Demerara sugar and press into the surface. Bake in the preheated oven for 30 minutes, until golden and cooked. Remove from the oven and, using a sharp knife, mark into portions, then leave to cool on the tin.

Shaping the dough.

Ingredients

50g/2oz hazelnuts, toasted
100g/4oz unsalted butter
50g/2oz caster sugar
125g/4 ½ oz plain flour
25g/1oz Demerara sugar

Sprinkling the Demerara sugar over the dough.

Almond Fingers

Ingredients

75g/3oz ground almonds

75g/3oz caster sugar

1 egg white

¼ teaspoon almond essence

Making the dough.

Preheat the oven to 180°C/350°F/Gas mark 4. In a mixing bowl, stir together the ground almonds and sugar. Add a little egg white and mix. Continue to do this until the mixture holds together in a stiff dough. Stir in the almond essence. Spoon the mixture into a piping bag and pipe the mixture in 5cm/2in lengths on to a baking tray lined with silicone paper or baking parchment, allowing room for them to spread. Bake for approximately 12–15 minutes until golden. Cool on the tray for 10 minutes then transfer to a cooling rack. Once fully cooled, store in an airtight container until ready to serve.

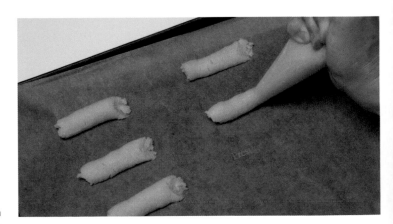

Piping the mixture on to a baking tray.

Mocha Biscotti

Preheat the oven to 180°C/350°F/Gas mark 4. Roughly chop the chocolate, then place in a blender or food processor with the cocoa, espresso powder and 25g of the sugar. Blend until you have a coarse mixture. Beat the remaining sugar with the butter then add the chocolate mixture and beat again. Stir in the egg a little at a time until it is all incorporated. Stir in the flour and mix thoroughly. Using lightly floured hands divide the mixture in half. Shape each half into a log

Ingredients

50g/2oz dark chocolate
1 tablespoon cocoa
2 teaspoons espresso
   powder
75g/3oz soft brown sugar
75g/3oz unsalted butter
1 egg, beaten
175g/6oz self raising flour,
   plus a little for dusting

Blend until you have a coarse mixture.

shape approximately 5cmcm/2in thick. Place the two logs on to a baking tray lined with silicone or baking parchment, allowing room for them to spread. Cook in the preheated oven for 20 minutes. Remove from the oven and slice each log diagonally into 1cm/ ½ in slices. Return the slices to the oven for a further 15 minutes, turning them halfway through. Cool on a wire rack. Store in an airtight container until ready to serve.

Shaping the mixture on a baking tray.

Brandy Snaps

Preheat the oven to 190°C/375°F/Gas mark 5. Sift the flour and ginger together on to a plate. Gently heat the butter, sugar, syrup and honey in a saucepan until melted. Add the flour and ginger and stir to mix. Line two baking sheets with baking parchment or silicone paper. Place teaspoonfuls of the mixture, spaced well apart, on to the prepared baking sheets and cook for approximately 10 minutes until golden. You will need to cook these in batches. Remove from the oven and wait 1–2 minutes until they are firm enough to handle. Then working

Ingredients

50g/2oz plain flour
½ teaspoon ground ginger
50g/2oz butter
150g/5oz caster sugar
1 tablespoon syrup
1 tablespoon runny honey

Adding the flour and ginger to the melted butter mix.

quickly, lift each one and shape as required. If they harden too quickly place them back in the oven for a couple of minutes to soften. If you want baskets, shape over an upturned glass; if you want tubes, roll around the handle of a wooden spoon; for cones, make firm cone shapes out of several layers of baking parchment and use as a mould. Continue to work in this way, cooking and shaping the mixture in batches, until all the mixture has been used up. Store in an airtight container until ready to serve.

Shaping the mixture around a wooden spoon handle.

Coconut Tuille

Preheat the oven to 190°C/375°F/Gas mark 5. Line two baking sheets with baking parchment or silicone paper. Beat the egg in a mixing bowl, then add the remaining ingredients. Mix thoroughly. Place spoonfuls of the mixture spaced well apart on the prepared baking sheets, spreading them thinly into round shapes. You will need to cook them in batches. Bake them in the preheated oven for 10–12 minutes, until they are turning golden. Remove from the oven and then, working quickly, lift each one and shape as required. If they harden too quickly, place them back in the oven for a couple of minutes to soften. If you want baskets, shape over an upturned glass; if you want tubes, roll around the handle of a wooden spoon; for cones, make firm cone shapes out of several layers of baking parchment and use as a mould. Continue to work in this way, cooking and shaping the mixture in batches, until all the mixture has been used up. Store in an airtight container until ready to serve.

Ingredients

- 1 egg
- 50g/2oz caster sugar
- 25g/1oz melted butter
- 25g/1oz plain flour
- 50g/2oz desiccated coconut

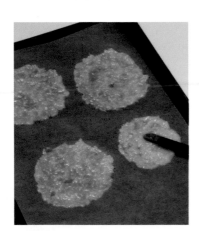

Spreading the mixture on a baking tray.

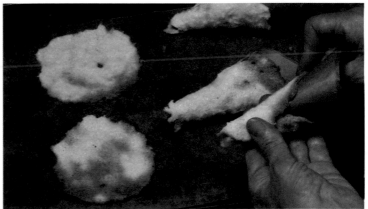

Shaping the mixture around parchment cones.

Coffee Meringue Nests.

Preheat the oven to 140°C/275°F/Gas mark 1. Line two baking sheets with baking parchment. On to the baking parchment draw four 10cm/4in circles with pencil, then turn the parchment over so that the circles are still visible but the pencil will not come off on to the meringues. In a large mixing bowl, whisk the egg whites until they form stiff peaks. Add the sugar a tablespoon at a time, whisking well between each addition. Add the coffee with the last addition of sugar and whisk. The mixture should be stiff and glossy. Place a large spoonful of the mixture into the centre of each circle and, using the back of the spoon, push the mixture out to the edges of the circle, raising the mixture up at the edges, so creating a nest. Bake in the oven for 2 hours, then turn the oven off and allow to cool in the oven. Once cooled, remove from the oven and store in an airtight container until ready to use.

Ingredients

2 egg whites

100g/4oz caster sugar

1 teaspoon espresso coffee powder

Adding the espresso powder to the meringue mix.

Shaping the meringue nests.

Apricot & Hazelnut Biscotti

Preheat the oven to 180°C/350°F/Gas mark 4. In a large mixing bowl sift the flour and baking powder and stir in the sugar. Add half the beaten egg and stir. Add the remaining egg a little at a time until you have a stiff dough (you may not need all the egg). Add the apricots, hazelnuts and orange zest, kneading well to mix. Turn the mixture out on to a clean surface and with lightly floured hands shape into two logs approximately 5cm/2in in diameter. Place each log on to a baking sheet lined with baking parchment or silicone paper, leaving space between them to spread. Cook for 25 minutes or until golden and firm to the touch. Reduce the oven temperature to 140°C/275°F/Gas mark 1. Remove from the oven and allow to cool for 10 minutes, then cut into 1–2cm (½–3/4in) slices diagonally. Place back on the baking sheets and cook for a further 20 minutes, turning halfway through. Cool on a wire rack. Store in an airtight container.

Kneading the ingredients to form a dough.

Ingredients

175g/6oz plain flour
1 teaspoon baking powder
175g/6oz caster sugar
1 large egg, beaten
100g/4oz dried ready-to-eat apricots, chopped
1 orange, zested
75g/3oz hazelnuts, toasted and chopped

Slicing the part-cooked biscotti.

Hazelnut Macaroons

Preheat the oven to 180°C/350°F/Gas mark 4. Finely grind the hazelnuts in a food processor or blender. It is better to do this in short bursts as you do not want the mixture to becoming oily (and this can happen quite quickly if it is over-processed). Mix the hazelnuts and caster sugar together in a bowl. Add the egg white a little at a time, mixing well between each addition. Ideally you need a very stiff dough, so you may not need to add all the egg white. Once you have reached the right consistency, place heaped teaspoons of the mixture on to a baking tray lined with baking parchment or silicone paper. Bake in the preheated oven for approximately 15 minutes. Cool on the tray for 5 minutes then lift off and continue to cool on a wire rack before transferring to an airtight container until ready to use.

Grinding the hazelnuts in a food processor.

Ingredients

75g/3oz hazelnuts

100g/4oz caster sugar

1 egg white

Spooning the mixture on to a baking tray.

SAUCES

Chocolate Sauce (Banana Split)

Put all the ingredients in a saucepan and heat gently until melted and fully combined. Then serve either hot or cold.

Serving suggestion:

To make a banana split: take one ripe banana and split lengthways, fill with scoops of ice cream of your choice and then drizzle over chocolate sauce. You can finish with chopped toasted nuts, glacé cherries or hundreds and thousands if you like.

Ingredients

150g/5oz dark chocolate
25g/1oz butter
1 tablespoon golden syrup
150ml/¼ pt single cream

Adding the cream to the saucepan.

Heating the ingredients until everything has melted.

Vanilla Cream (Cappuccino)

Ingredients
1 egg white
25g/1oz caster sugar
1 teaspoon vanilla essence
150ml/ ¼ pt double cream

Adding sugar to the egg whites.

Whisk the egg white in a mixing bowl until it forms soft peaks. Add the sugar a spoonful at a time, whisking between each addition until the mixture is stiff and glossy. Whip the cream and vanilla essence together until the cream holds its shape. Gently fold the sweetened egg white into the cream. Serve.

Serving suggestion:
Use to top coffee ice cream and sprinkle lightly with a little cocoa to give a cappuccino effect.

Folding the egg white into the cream.

Hot Fudge Sauce

Gently heat the sugar in a small saucepan, stirring from time to time with a wooden spoon, until melted and starting to caramelise. Remove from the heat and stir in the butter, syrup and cream. Then gently reheat, stirring until thoroughly mixed. Remove from the heat and serve. This is also delicious cold.

Heating the sugar in a saucepan.

Ingredients

100g/4oz caster sugar

100g/4oz butter

1 tablespoon syrup

5 tablespoons double cream

Adding the cream to the caramelised sugar.

Index

Acknowledgements

I would like to thank Gaggia for the loan of their "Gelatiera" model, which was a great help in making so many of the ice creams in this book. I would also like to thank Braun for supplying the Multiquick which was invaluable in the preparation of many of the recipes. Thanks also to Magi Mix for the loan of two of their ice cream makers.

Raspberry (Peach Melba)

Place the ingredients in a pan with 6 tablespoons of water and cook over a gentle heat until boiling, stirring from time to time. Remove from the heat. Set a sieve over a bowl and pour the mixture into the sieve pressing down on it with a wooden spoon to make sure as much as possible goes into the bowl. Discard the pips that have caught in the sieve. Stir the purée that has collected in the bowl and leave to cool. Use as required.

Serving suggestion:
To make a peach melba, skin one peach per person, split in half and remove the stone. Add a scoop of vanilla ice cream and drizzle over some of the raspberry sauce, then serve.

Heating the ingredients in a saucepan.

Ingredients
200g/7oz raspberries
4 tablespoons raspberry jam
½ lemon, juiced

Sieving the raspberry mix to form a purée.

Coffee

Pour 150ml/ ¼ pt of boiling water over the coffee and leave to stand for 5 minutes. Set a fine mesh strainer over a bowl and pour in the coffee, pressing down on the grounds to get as much of the coffee liquid into the bowl as possible. Add the cream and sugar and stir until dissolved, then serve. Delicious poured over vanilla ice cream.

Ingredients
3 tablespoons ground
coffee
25g/1oz granulated sugar
150ml/ ¼ pt double cream

Pouring boiling water over the coffee grounds.

Adding the cream and sugar to the coffee.